Animal
Hide and Seek

FIRST EDITION
Series Editor Deborah Lock; **Art Editor** Clare Shedden; **US Editor** John Searcy; **Production** Angela Graef;
Picture Researcher Julia Harris-Voss; **DTP Designer** Almudena Díaz; **Jacket Designer** Emy Manby;
Reading Consultant Linda Gambrell, PhD

THIS EDITION
Editorial Management by Oriel Square
Produced for DK by WonderLab Group LLC
Jennifer Emmett, Erica Green, Kate Hale, *Founders*

Editors Grace Hill Smith, Libby Romero, Michaela Weglinski;
Photography Editors Kelley Miller, Annette Kiesow, Nicole DiMella; **Managing Editor** Rachel Houghton;
Designers Project Design Company; **Researcher** Michelle Harris; **Copy Editor** Lori Merritt;
Indexer Connie Binder; **Proofreader** Larry Shea; **Reading Specialist** Dr. Jennifer Albro;
Curriculum Specialist Elaine Larson

Published in the United States by DK Publishing
1745 Broadway, 20th Floor, New York, NY 10019

Copyright © 2023 Dorling Kindersley Limited
DK, a Division of Penguin Random House LLC
23 24 25 26 27 10 9 8 7 6 5 4 3 2 1
001–333442–Apr/2023

All rights reserved.
Without limiting the rights under the copyright reserved
above, no part of this publication may be reproduced, stored
in or introduced into a retrieval system, or transmitted, in any
form, or by any means (electronic, mechanical, photocopying,
recording, or otherwise), without the prior written permission
of the copyright owner.
Published in Great Britain by Dorling Kindersley Limited

A catalog record for this book
is available from the Library of Congress.
HC ISBN: 978-0-7440-6749-1
PB ISBN: 978-0-7440-6750-7

DK books are available at special discounts when purchased
in bulk for sales promotions, premiums, fundraising, or
educational use. For details, contact: DK Publishing Special Markets,
1745 Broadway, 20th Floor, New York, NY 10019
SpecialSales@dk.com

Printed and bound in China

The publisher would like to thank the following for their kind permission to reproduce their images:
a=above; c=center; b=below; l=left; r=right; t=top; b/g=background
Dreamstime.com: Aleksey Alekhin 18, Andamanse 19, Steve Byland 12–13; **Shutterstock.com:** Kurit afshen 23br, frank60 25crb,
Brian Lasenby 24, Stu Porter 29tr, RRichard29 10crb, Richard Seeley 10t
Cover images: *Front:* **Dreamstime.com:** Terriana; **Shutterstock.com:** Jim Cumming b, clb;
Back: **Dreamstime.com:** Glolyla cra, Pavel Naumov cl
All other images © Dorling Kindersley

For the curious
www.dk.com

Level 3

Animal Hide and Seek

Penny Smith

DK

Contents

6	Camouflage
9	Wild Boars
10	Snowshoe Hare
12	American Dipper
14	Chinchillas
16	Butterfly
19	Pipefish
21	Decorator Crabs
22	Chameleon

25	Stick Insect
26	Zebras
28	Meerkats
30	Glossary
31	Index
32	Quiz

Camouflage

In the wild, some animals eat other animals for food. The animals hope their enemies do not see them. Some animals are covered in patterns and colors. They look like their surroundings. This is called camouflage.

comma butterfly

green tree frog

woodcock

Wild Boars

Here is a family of wild boars. A baby boar might make a tasty meal for a wolf. The babies have striped coats. They are hard to see.

Snowshoe Hare

In the summer, the snowshoe hare has red-brown fur. In the winter, its fur grows thick and white. The hare crouches on the snow. An owl flies overhead. It does not see the still and silent hare.

Changing Colors
Snowshoe hares aren't the only animals that change color with the seasons. More than 20 different birds and mammals change from brown to white throughout the year.

American Dipper

This American dipper waits near a mountain stream. It is looking for insects to eat. Its blue-gray feathers make it hard to see against the water.

Chinchillas

The gray fur of the chinchillas keeps them hidden against the rocks and stones. Owls, foxes, and snakes do not notice them there.

Butterfly

When this butterfly's wings are closed, they are dark to blend in with the shadows. When it flutters, its wings look like the eyes of a big animal. This startles an enemy. The butterfly has time to fly away.

A Bright Warning
Many butterflies are toxic because of what they ate as caterpillars. Their bright colors and patterns warn enemies not to eat them.

Pipefish

This pipefish beats its tiny fins and swims among the branches of underwater plants. Can you see it? It is not easy to find.

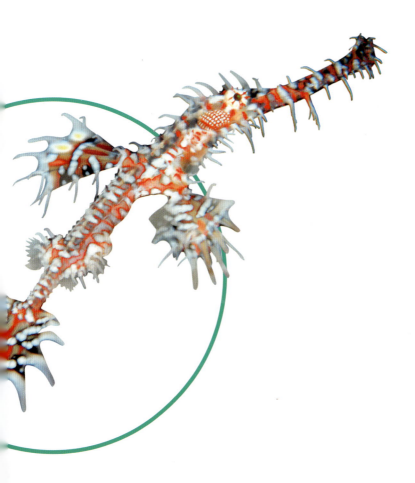

Decorator Crabs

These decorator crabs hook seaweed, stones, and small sea creatures onto their bodies. The crabs are hidden. As the crabs grow, they crawl out of their shells. They put the old decorations onto their new shells.

Chameleon

In the rainforest, the chameleon is as green as the branch it sits on. It can change color to match its surroundings. It is hard for enemies to find.

Matching the Vibe
Chameleons can change their color based on the temperature, their environment, and even their moods! When a chameleon gets angry, it can turn yellow, orange, and red.

Stick Insect

Can you see the stick insect? It is the same color and shape as the twigs on a plant. The stick insect's eggs look like seeds.

A Living Stick
Stick insects are also known as walking sticks. This is because they look like small sticks. They can even move back and forth like a twig caught in the breeze.

25

Zebras

In the African grasslands, zebras graze together for safety. Their striped coats make it hard to tell one zebra from another.

Lions have trouble seeing which one to attack. The zebras' stripes can also keep biting flies from landing on them.

Finding Mama
A baby zebra can tell its mother apart from other zebras by looking at her stripes. She has her own special stripe pattern that the baby remembers.

Meerkats

In the dry desert, a meerkat sits up and sniffs the air. An eagle flies overhead. The silver-brown color of the meerkats' fur makes it hard for the eagle to see them.

Ring the Alarm
When meerkats are on guard duty, they have six different calls. Each call has to do with the level of nearby danger. They also have a call that gives the group an "all-clear" sign.

When animals camouflage themselves, it's almost like playing hide-and-seek with their enemies. Next time you're in nature, you might spot an animal hiding in plain sight!

Glossary

Camouflage
[KAM-uh-flahj]
A way for animals to disguise their appearance to blend in with their surroundings

Chameleon
[kuh-MEEL-yun]
A scaly lizard that can change colors and move its eyes in different directions

Eagle
A large bird that hunts and eats smaller animals

Hare
A large rabbit with long ears, short tails, and long hind legs

Insect
A small animal with three pairs of legs and one or two pairs of wings

Meerkat
A small mammal that lives in a large group in the southern tip of Africa

Owl
A kind of bird with large eyes and strong talons that usually hunts at night

Pipefish
A long, slender fish in the same family as sea horses

Wild Boar
A hairy, wild pig with a black or brown coat that comes from Europe and Asia

Index

alarm calls 28
American dipper 12
baby animals 9, 27
biting flies 27
butterflies 7, 16, 17
camouflage 6, 29
caterpillars 17
chameleons 22, 23
changing colors 10, 22, 23
chinchillas 14
comma butterfly 7
decorator crabs 21
eagle 28
eggs 25
enemies 6, 16, 17, 22, 29
feathers 12
flies 27
foxes 14
fur 10, 14, 28

green tree frog 7
insects 12, 25
lions 27
meerkats 28
owls 10, 14
pipefish 19
shells 21
snakes 14
snowshoe hare 10
stick insects 25
striped animals 9, 26–27
walking sticks 25
warning colors 17
wild boars 9
wings 16
wolf 9
woodcock 7
zebras 26–27

Quiz

Answer the questions to see what you have learned. Check your answers in the key below.

1. Why do some animals use camouflage?
2. Why does the snowshoe hare's fur change to white in the winter?
3. What do the spots on a butterfly's wings look like?
4. Why do chameleons change color?
5. How can a baby zebra find its mother among other zebras?

1. So their enemies will not see them 2. To blend in with the snow 3. The eyes of a big animal 4. To match their temperature, environment, or mood 5. By looking for its mother's stripes